The Shell Book

By Sandra Romashko

The complete guide to collecting and identifying
with a special section
on starfish and other collectable sea creatures.

Fourth Edition

𝒲indward Publishing, Inc.

105 NE 25th St.   P.O. Box 371005   Miami, Fl. 33137

15 17 19 20 18 16 14

Printed in the United States of America.
Library of Congress Catalog Card No. 76-360976
ISBN 0-89317-000-3

Contents

UNIVALVES

Generally augers are found on beaches or live on mud flats. One of the less common species, the Flame Auger, can be found by trails left on mud in which they are found buried. Atlantic augers are more common and generally available to collectors.

Found in shallow waters and grass flats, the heavy shelled bonnet is frequently washed up on beaches intact.

These shells can be found on the beach and as living specimens on mud flats and reefs. Some species are very delicate and seldom are found intact.

Carriers derive their name from their habit of picking up other pieces of shells, coral and other calcium-laden debris, which they then incorporate as part of their own shell.

Live conchs, camouflaged by a brown periosteum covering the shell, are found in beds and groups in shallow waters. The conch is a staple of the Bahamas and considered very good eating. However, regardless of size, the conch is not fully developed until the flaring lip appears. It is prey to both man and the horse conch.

There are hundreds of species of cones and these very colorful shells are common to collectors. Live cones should be handled with respect since they contain a barbed harpoon-like proboscis which injects a paralyzing toxin to its prey, and delivers a painful sting to man. Cones are found under sponges, rocks, and in the sand.

Cowries can be found in daylight hiding under rocks and in crevices. At night they search for their food on rocks and other protrusions. Cowries found on the beach are usually less colorful than the live specimen, since the mantle no longer protects the shell and it is therefore bleached by exposure to the sun.

These specimens are found in shallow waters and mud flats. Different species will contain one to several rows of spines, or some, no spines at all. Many color combinations exist, including albino.

Distorsios are found on rocky flats and crevices, usually covered by heavy marine growth.

Drills are extensively destructive to other mollusks, particularly bivalves.

These shells burrow in sand while feeding. Their habitat is identified by sand collars which are built to incubate their egg masses.

Fusinus can be found washed up on beaches or live on mud flats.

Helmets can be found on the sand in shallow water with most of the shell buried below the surface of the water. These large univalves feed on sea urchins and other members of the sea urchin family.

The horse conch is a carnivorous univalve which can be found in mud flats or reefs. They can be found in color variations from orange to brown, and sometimes albino.

These are prized and expensive shells. The main supply is found by dredging off coastal waters.

These small colorful shells are sand burrowers and are found in tidal pools, usually in generous quantities.

Moon shells feed on other univalves and can be found burrowed in the sand or on the beach when they are washed up by the waters. They plant their eggs in sand collars, which identify the area they inhabit.

Generally murex are found on rocks and coral in shallow waters. They are characterized by their irregular and spiny shapes. The murex is carnivorous and lives off other shells and minute life.

Like the moon snails, naticas feed on univalves and plant their eggs in sand collars. They are also found burrowed in the sand or washed up on the beach.

Nerites are plentiful and can be found on water-washed sea walls, rocks, and in crevices.

Nutmegs are found on the beaches or live on mud flats.

When live, the mantle and foot of the olive surrounds the shell and keeps it polished to a high gloss which is even apparent in dead specimens. The species is prevalent and found buried in the sand.

Periwinkles can be found on the beach, and as live specimens on mud flats, sea walls, rocks and reefs.

These very colorful shells are also very fragile and the dye which gives them their color will also stain your clothes. They are often washed ashore in groups which are held together at sea by bubble-like floats.

Rock shells are generally found in shallow waters, on rocks or coral.

These snails have very colorful and distinctive mantles and therefore they are especially beautiful when captured or observed alive. One of the most popular species is the Flamingo Tongue, whose mantle looks like a leopard skin.

Living star shells can be found on rocky crevices and sea walls. A whitish oval operculum is characteristic of these shells.

Sun-dials can be found washed up on beaches, but they are somewhat rare. The sun-dial's common name is characteristic of its appearance.

These shells can be found in rocky crevices or mixed in with dead coral. They are often heavily coated with deposits and require careful cleaning.

Tritons can be found living on the reefs or in the sand. They are carnivorous and feed on starfish. The univalve grows quite large and exists in many beautiful color variations.

Trivias can be found in abundance washed up on beaches.

Tulips are carnivors and feed on other mollusks. Their colors range from dark brown to reds and oranges.

In spite of their bulky appearance, tuns are quite light and are occasionally found washed up on beaches. Live specimens can be found on underwater reefs.

Turbans can be found in rocky crevices or mixed in with dead coral. They also require careful cleaning, since they are often coated with deposits.

Turrets can be found washed up on beaches or live on mud flats.

These shells are found washed up on beaches or on mud flats.

Volutes are quite rare and are highly prized as specimens. They are sometimes found on beaches off coastal waters where dredging has thrown them ashore.

Whelks were used as food, houseware and weapons by Indians in Florida and are found in tribal burial grounds. They can be found live in shallow waters and mud flats.

Worm shells are quite abundant and can be found on beaches, reefs, and mud flats.

BIVALVES

These very delicate specimens are found buried deep in mud banks.

Arks are characterized by their heavy shells which lack any significant amount of color.

Bittersweets are interestingly colored and are found easily.

These are perhaps the most commonly recognized shells. They are easily found in abundance on beaches or buried in the sand.

Cockles are often found washed up on beaches; live specimens live in shallow waters in constant motion with the movement of the sand.

These bivalves are found in a wide variety of colors growing on sea walls and pilings. They are sometimes found growing together in clusters.

PARTS OF THE SHELL

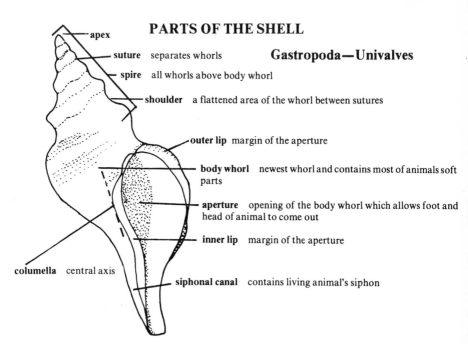

Gastropoda—Univalves

apex

suture separates whorls

spire all whorls above body whorl

shoulder a flattened area of the whorl between sutures

outer lip margin of the aperture

body whorl newest whorl and contains most of animals soft parts

aperture opening of the body whorl which allows foot and head of animal to come out

inner lip margin of the aperture

columella central axis

siphonal canal contains living animal's siphon

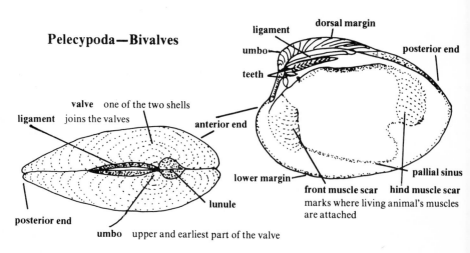

Pelecypoda—Bivalves

ligament

dorsal margin

umbo

posterior end

teeth

valve one of the two shells

ligament joins the valves

anterior end

lower margin

pallial sinus

front muscle scar hind muscle scar marks where living animal's muscles are attached

lunule

posterior end

umbo upper and earliest part of the valve

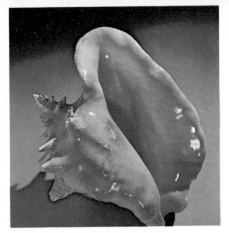

Natural History

The Shell is the exoskeleton of animals categorized in the phylum *Mollusca*. Mollusks have inhabited the earth for over 600 million years and can be found throughout the globe on every continent and ocean, in all environments — even above the snow-line in the Himalayas. However, most prefer warm climates and gentle seas. The Florida coasts, ocean and gulf, and the Caribbean provide a lush hunting ground for The Shell Collector.

The mollusk shell is the product of the mantle, a fold of muscular flesh which covers the back and sides of the animal like a skirt. The mantle has many pores through which the animal secretes a thin limy substance which solidifies quickly into a thin layer. Layers are built up one upon the other, often crosswise, until the mass is built up into the shell. Often, the surface is "final coated" by the animal with a thin procelain-like finish. The outer edges of the mantle continue to secrete, allowing the shell to grow in width and length, while pores in the mantle within the shell add to the thickness of the shell and also perform any necessary repairs.

In some species the interior walls are made of alternating layers of lime and horny tissue — shingle like lime crystals. When light is reflected from the edges of these microscopic shingles, the luster produced is known as mother-of-pearl.

The family *Mollusca* contains over 50,000 species, of which the common members belong to the following classes.

Gastropoda — univalves (single shells) or snails.

Pelecypoda — bivalves (two shells) such as clams, oysters, or scallops.

Cephalopoda — squid, octopus.

Yes, the octopus too is a mollusk, but obviously the Shell Collector is concerned basically with univalves and bivalves.

Univalves are the most populous class of mollusks, generally curled, with the fleshy part of the animal secured by one strong muscle to the top of the shell. Univalves, or snails, have a foot which is used for locomotion, a head, and eat by means of a radula — a file-like tongue coated with sharp teeth — which may reach twice the length of the body. Many bear an operculum for protection — a horny shield that closes like a trap door when the animal is inside. With the radula univalves can bore holes in other shells, usually the bivalves. A snail, *Urosalpinx cinerea*, the "oyster drill" cuts a hole in one side of the bivalve and inserts a tube-like projection and sucks the victim's flesh. The members of the *Conidae* genus are the deadliest of all mollusks, and live specimens should be handled with respect. Their poisonous spear-like radula penetrates its victim and acts on the nervous system, paralyzing the prey. The sting of *Conus geographus* once killed a man.

Bivalves account for some 10,000 species of which the quahog, *Mercenaria mercenaria,* and the edible oyster, *Crassostrea virginica,* are among the most familiar. Bivalves have two shells hinged together and the fleshy part of the animal i connected to the hinge by one or two muscles. Most bivalves live on microscopic lif drawn towards the stomach by water currents generated by the vibrating of filaments (cilia) on the gills.

The Coquina clams, *Dorax variablis,* Florida's most abundant bivalves, survive by means of two siphons projecting from the mouth of the shell. One siphon inhales water bearing oxygen and food and the other expels water along with waste materials. Incidentally, the shells of the Coquinas were used by the Spaniards 300 years ago to build Castillo de San Marcus in St. Augustine, Florida. Even today the shells of bivalves are used commercially, as a soft limestone for building roads and homes.

Bivalves, like univalves, have a foot which in many species is used as a digging tool as well as for locomotion, scallops can leap and swim, and other bivalves move. Spats (young oysters) are mobile for a brief period until the oyster finds a place to anchor itself with its foot where it lives its entire adult life without moving. Spat's chances of survival are so small that the female oyster produces a hundred million eggs at a time, of which only a few develop.

Mollusks lay eggs, but reproduction among the different bivalves varies greatly. Some retain the eggs inside the parent until ready to hatch. Oysters emit a spray of eggs into a sperm cloud ejected by a nearby male. Some scallops, clams and shipworms are hermaphroditic. Some, like the oyster, change sex during their lifetime.

Collecting Shells

The waters of Florida and the Caribbean provide excellent sites for beach combing for shells. The gentle waters wash many perfect specimens up on the wide sand flats in these areas. The best time for beach combing is at low tide at its ebb. Especially good are tides from a new full moon which are very low. Mollusks such as Volutes spend much time in sand and can be more readily found during an ebbing tide. During their brief emergence from the sand, Volutes leave a trail an inch wide and sometimes 20 feet long stopping abruptly where the animal has burrowed again. Beaches and shores will often contain live, numerous specimens after a storm.

High tide will sometimes wash fragile shells ashore along with seaweed and other debris. The tide will also expose the furious Coquina which scramble to bury themselves in the sand when they are washed up by waves or left behing by the low tide.

Skin diving provides a means of collecting live and perfect specimens, which are seldom found on shore. These shells are often more brilliant in color since they have not been exposed to sunlight or harsh elements, and since they contain live or newly dead animals.

In addition to aesthetic value, many shells have intrinsic value depending on their condition, supply, and demand. "The Glory of the Sea", *Conus gloriamaris,* is one of the rarest and most expensive shells in the world. One of 70 known shells is pictured.

"Glory of the Sea",
Conus gloriamaris.

Cleaning Shells

All shells require some cleaning to enhance their natural beauty. Live shells or those which still contain the dead animal require additional attention. Boiling the mollusks (2 minutes for a delicate specimen to 30 minutes for a heartier one) will kill the animal which then can be removed with forceps or tweezers by applying a steady twisting motion so that the entire animal comes free.

If the anchor muscle breaks off and remains in the shell, a few drops of alcohol added to the shell will shrink and remove the remaining matter in a few days.

A "natural" method for removing flesh from the shell, and one that is recommended for fragile shells, is the "ant cleaning system." Leave the shell exposed outdoors or lightly buried for about a week. It will be stripped clean of any flesh.

Shells free from any animal matter should then be soaked 8-12 hours in an undiluted solution of bleach to dissolve any remaining flesh and eliminate any odor. Shells which have become encrusted with barnacles, calcium deposits, or algae can be cleaned with a dilute solution of muriatic acid. The acid should be applied in small quantities and then quickly rinsed off. Muriatic acid is very caustic and hands and clothing should be protected. A final coating of baby or olive oil will preserve the color and sheen.

Bivalves must be cleaned carefully so as not to break the hinge. Clear glue or shellac lightly applied to the hinge will strengthen it. Professional collectors will replace the operculum after cleaning by gluing it to a wad of cotton or tissue placed into the opening of the shell. After cleaning, a bivalve can be soaked in a solution of equal parts glycerin and water and tied shut until dry which will allow the shell to stay shut; dead bivalves will normally be in the open position.

Once the shells have been cleaned, they can be beautifully displayed almost anywhere — but they should be kept from sunlight since their intense color will soon be bleached out.

Key to Abbreviations

F Florida	**T** Texas
SF South Florida	**K** Florida Keys
SEF Southeast Florida	**KW** Key West
FEC Florida East Coast	**B** Bahamas
NF Northern Florida	**BR** Bermuda
EF Eastern Florida	**Y** Yucatan
WF Western Florida	**SC** Southern Caribbean
G Gulf of Mexico	**CC** Cape Cod
C Caribbean	**V** Virginia
WC Western Caribbean	**GA** Greater Antilles
NC North Carolina	**LA** Lesser Antilles
WI West Indies	

Conchs

Lamp Conch, *Xancus angulatus,*
7-14", B, KW, Y, BR, Cuba.

Pink Conch or Queen Conch, *Strombus gigas,* 6-12", B, SEF, WI.

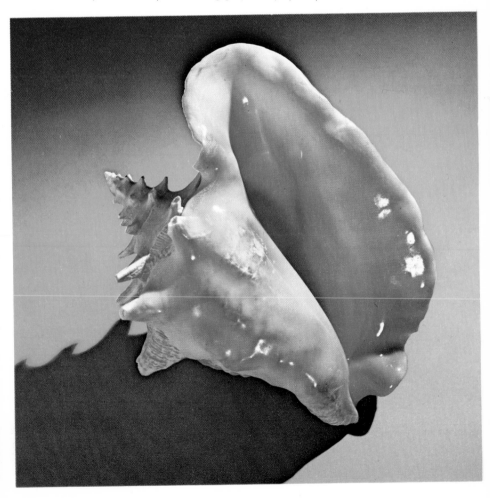

Conchs and Carrier Shells

Hawk-wing Conch, *Strombus raninus,* 2-4'', SEF,WI.

Rooster-tail Conch, *Strombus gallus,* 4-6'', SEF, WI.

Milk Conch, *Strombus costatus,* 4-7'', SEF, WI.

Fighting Conch, *Strombus pugilis,* 3-4'', F, WI.

Atlantic Carrier Shell, *Xenophora conchyliophora,* 2'', NC to KW, WI.

Strombus gigas, Juvenile form, 3-6'', SEF, WI.

Purple variety, *Strombus pugilis.*

Caribbean Carrier Shell, *Xenophora caribaeum,* 2'', WI, C.

Strombus raninus nanus, 1-1½'', F, WI.

Crown Conchs

Top Three,
King's Crown or Crown Conch,
Melongena corona, 2-4", F, G.

West Indian Crown Conch,
(young specimen, lacks spines),
Melongena melongena, 3-6",
WI.

Horse Conchs

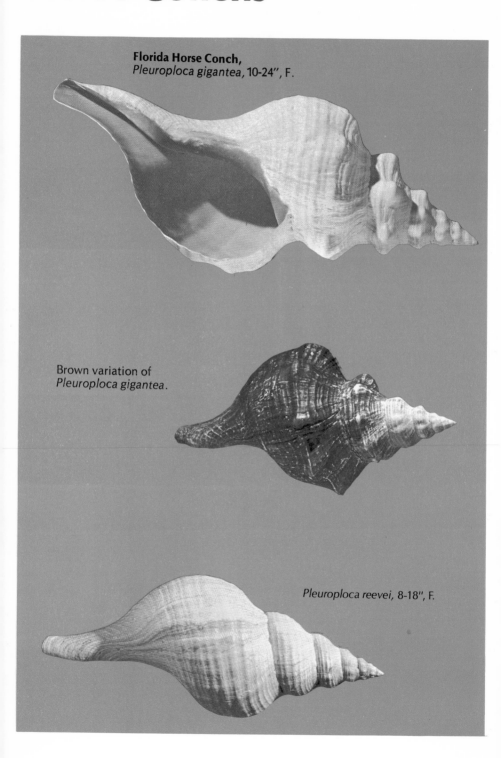

Florida Horse Conch,
Pleuroploca gigantea, 10-24″, F.

Brown variation of
Pleuroploca gigantea.

Pleuroploca reevei, 8-18″, F.

Carved Star Shell, *Astraea caelata,* 2-3", SEF, WI.

Astraea caelata, juvenile form.

Star Arene, *Arene cruentata,* ¼", SEF, WI.

American Star Shell, *Astraea americana,* 1-1½", SEF.

Green Star Shell, *Astraea tuber,* 1-2", SEF, WI.

Long-spined Star Shell, *Astraea phoebia,* 2-2½", SEF, WI.

Astraea phoebia spinulosa. 2-2½", SEF, WI.

17

Tritons

Triton Trumpet,
Charonia variegata,
12-18″, SEF, WI.

Angular Triton, *Cymatium femorale,*
3-7″, SEF, WI.

Tiger Triton, *Cymatium tigrinus,*
Broderip, 4-5″, WC.

1. *Cymatium costatum*, 3-4", NC to WI.
2. **Atlantic Hairy Triton,** *Cymatium pileare*, 1½-3", NC to SEF, WI.
3. **Dog-head Triton,** *Cymatium caribbaeum*, 1½-2½" SEF, WI.
4. **Poulsen's Triton,** *Cymatium poulseni*, 2-3", F, WI.
5. **Gold-mouthed Triton,** *Cymatium chlorostomum*, 1-2½", SEF, WI.
6. **Knobbed Triton,** *Cymatium muricinum*, 1-2", SEF, BR, WI.
7. **Kreb's Triton,** *Cymatium krebsi*, 2-3", F to WI.
8. **Dwarf Hairy Triton,** *Cymatium vespaceum*, 1-1½", SEF to WI.

Cowries

1. **Measled Cowry,** Cypraea zebra, 2-3½", SEF, WI.
2. **Atlantic Deer Cowry,** Cypraea cervus, 3-5", SF, C.
3. **Atlantic Yellow Cowry,** Cypraea spurca acicularis, ½-1¼", SF, Y, WI.
4. **Mouse Cowry,** Cypraea mus, 2", SC.
5. **Atlantic Gray Cowry,** Cypraea cinerea, ¾-1½", SEF, WI.

Distorsios

Atlantic Distorsio, Distorsio clathrata, 1-2½", F, G, C.

McGinty's Distorsio, Distorsio constricta mcgintyi, 1-2", NC to SF.

Nerites and Sun-dials
Purple Sea-snail

1. **Common Sun-dial,** *Architectonica nobilis,* 1-2", NC, F, T, WI.
2. **Bleeding Tooth,** *Nerita peloronta,* 1", F, WI.
3. **Virgin Nerite,** *Neritina virginea,* ½", F, WI.
4. **Common Purple Sea-snail,** *Janthina janthina,* 1", Worldwide.
5. **Four toothed Nerite,** *Nerita versicolor,* ¾-1", F, WI.
6. **Zebra Nerite,** *Puperita pupa,* 1/3-½", SEF, WI.
7. **Keeled Sun-dial,** *Architectonica peracuta,* ¾", SEF, WI.
8. **Tessellate Nerite,** *Nerita tessellata,* ¾", F, WI.

Turbans and Top Shells

1. **Channeled Turban,** *Turbo canaliculatus,* 2-3″, K, WI.
2. **West Indian Top Shell** or **Megpie,** *Cittarium pica,* 2-4″, F, WI.
3. **Superb Gaza,** *Gaza superba,* 1-1½″, G to WI.
4. **Chestnut Turban,** *Turbo castaneus,* 1-1½″, F, WI.

1. **Sculptured Top Shell,** *Calliostoma euglyptum,* ¾″, NC to F, T.
2. **Chocolate-lined Top Shell,** *Calliostoma javanicum,* ¾-1″, K, WI.
3. **Jujube Top Shell,** *Calliostoma jujubinum,* ½-1¼″, K, B, WI.
4. *Calliostoma iris,* ½″, FEC.

King Helmet, *Cassis tuberosa,* 4-9″, SEF, WI.

Queen Helmet, *Cassis madagascariensis,* 4-9″, SEF, B, GA.

Tuns

Top:
Giant Tun Shell, *Tonna galea,* 5-7″, NC to F, G, WI.
Bottom:
Atlantic Partridge Tun, *Tonna maculosa,* 2-5″, SEF, WI.

Tulip Shells

Banded Tulip, *Fasciolaria hunteria,* 2-4″, F, G.

Branham's Tulip, *Fasciolaria branhamae,* 3-5″, G.

Color variation of *Fasciolaria hunteria.*

True Tulip, *Fasciolaria tulipa,* 3-5″, SF, WI.

Whelks

Turnip Whelk, *Busycon coarctatum*, 5″, G.

1. **Channeled Whelk,** *Busycon canaliculatum*, 5-7½″, CC to NF.
2. **Lightning Whelk,** rare right-handed specimen of *Busycon contrarium.*
3. **Knobbed Whelk,** *Busycon carica,* 4-8″, both coasts of Central Florida.
4. **Lightning Whelk or Left-handed Whelk,** *Busycon contrarium*, 4-16″, F, G.
5. **Pear Whelk,** *Busycon spiratum,* 3-4″, NC to F, G.

Sea-whip Snails

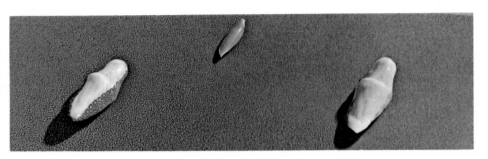

Flamingo Tongue,
Cyphoma gibbosum,
¾-1″, NC to SEF, WI.

Single-toothed Simnia,
Neosimnia uniplicata,
½-¾″, F, WI.

McGinty's Cyphoma,
Cyphoma mcgintyi,
¾-1¼″, K.

Frog Shells

Gaudy Frog Shell, *Bursa corrugata,* 2-3″,
SEF, C.

Granular Frog Shell, *Bursa granularis,*
1-2″, SEF, WI.

Bonnets

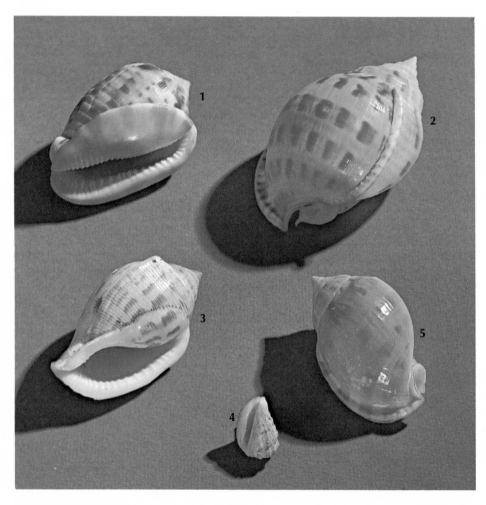

1. **Reticulated Cowrie-helmet,** *Cypraecassis testiculus,* 3″, SEF, BR, WI.
2. **Scotch Bonnet,** *Phalium granulatum,* 1½-3″, NC to G, WI.
3. **Royal Bonnet,** *Sconsia striata,* 1½-2½″, SEF, WI.
4. **Atlantic Wood-louse,** *Morum oniscus,* ¾-1″, SEF, WI.
5. **Smooth Scotch Bonnet,** *Phalium cicatricosum,* 1½-2″, SEF, C.

Fusinus and Augers

1. Turnip Spindle, *Fusinus timessus,* 3", G.
2. *Fusinus halistrepus,* 1½", G.
3. Flame Auger, *Terebra taurinum,* 4-6", SEF, G, WI.
4. Shiny Atlantic Auger, *Terebra hastata,* 1¼-1½", F, WI.
5. Coue's Spindle, *Fusinus couei,* 4", G.
6. Common Atlantic Auger, *Terebra dislocata,* 1½-2", V to F, WI.
7. Ornamented Spindle, *Fusinus eucosmius,* 3", G.
8. Gray Atlantic Auger, *Terebra cinerea,* 1-2", SEF, WI.
9. *Fusinus helenae,* 1½", G.

Murex and Rock Shells

Bequaert's Murex, *Murex bequaerti,* 1-2½", NC to KW.

Apple Murex, *Murex pomum,* 2-4½", F, WI.

Cabrit's Murex, *Murex cabriti,* 1-3", SF, LA.

Beau's Murex, *Murex beaui,* 3-5", G, WI.

Woodring's Murex, *Murex woodringi,* 2-3", C.

Lace Murex, *Murex florifer,* 1-3", F, WI.

Giant Eastern Murex, *Murex fulvescens,* 5-7", G, EF.

West Indian Murex, *Murex brevifrons,* 3-6", K, WI.

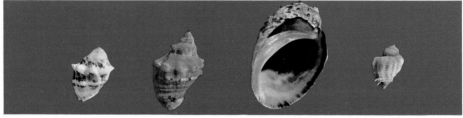

Deltoid Rock-Shell, *Thais deltoidea,* 1-2", F, BR, WI.

Florida Rock-Shell, *Thais haemastoma floridana,* 2-3", NC to F, C.

Wide-mouthed Purpura, *Purpura patula,* 2-3½", SEF, WI.

Short Coral-shell, *Coralliophila abbreviata,* ¾-1½", SEF, WI.

1. *Murex cailleti*, Petit, 2-4", SF, WI.
2. **Gold-mouthed Murex,** *Murex chrysostoma*, 1½-3", F, WI.
3. **Rose Murex,** *Murex recurvirostris rubidus*, 1-2", F, B.
4. *Murex recurvirostris sallasi*, 1-2", C.
5. **Pitted Murex,** *Murex cellulosus leviculus*, 1", EF.
6. **Hexagonal Murex,** *Muricopsis oxytatus.* 1½", K, WI.
7. *Coralliophila deburghiae*, Reeve, 1-1½", F.

8. *Murex mcgintyi*, 1", K, WI.
9. **Pitted Murex,** *Murex cellulosus*, 1", F, G, WI.
10. **Tryon's Murex,** *Murex tryoni*, 1-3", F, WI.
11. **Thick-lipped Drill,** *Eupleura caudata*, ½-1", CC to F.
12. **Tampa Drill Shell,** *Urosalpinx tampaensis*, ½-1", WF.
13. **False Drill Shell,** *Pseudoneptunea multangula*, Philippi, 1-1¼", F, WI.

Junonia

Junonia, *Scaphella junonia,* 5-6", F, G.

Naticas,
Moon and Ear Shells

1. **Common Nutmeg Shell,** *Cancellaria reticulata,* 1-1¾", NC to F.
2. **Bubble Shell,** *Bulla amygdala,* Brug, ¾-1", WF, WI.
3. **Brown-lined Paper Bubble Shell,** *Hydatina vesicaria,* 1-1½", SF, WI.
4. **Adele's Nutmeg,** *Cancellaria reticulata adelae,* 1-1½", K.
5. *Cancellaria tenera,* Philippi, 1-1¾", G.
6. **Paper Bubble Shell,** *Haminoea elegans,* 1/3", SEF, WI.
7. *Cancellaria conradiana,* 1-1¾", F.

◀ 1. **Shark's Eye,** *Polinices duplicatus,* 1-2½", F, G.
2. **Colorful Atlantic Natica,** *Natica canrena,* 1-2", F, WI.
3. **Brown Moon Shell,** *Polinices brunneus,* 1-2", SEF, WI.
4. **Morocco Natica,** *Natica marochiensis,* ½-1", F, WI.
5. **Maculated Baby's Ear,** *Sinum maculatum,* 1-2", Carolinas and West Coast of Florida.
6. **Livid Natica,** *Natica livida,* ½", SEF, C, BR.
7. **Milk Moon Shell,** *Polinices lacteus,* ¾-1½", NC, SEF, WI.
8. **Common Baby's Ear,** *Sinum perspectivum,* 1-2", V to F, G, WI.

Cones

Warty Cone, *Conus verrucosus,* ¾-1", SEF, WI.

Austin's Cone, *Conus austini,* 2-2½", Tortugas to Yucatan , WI.

Jasper Cone, *Conus iaspideus,* ½-¾", SF, WI.

Conus peali, ½-¾", SF, WI.

Clark's Cone, *Conus clarki,* 1-1½", G.

Conus perryae, ¾-1", F.

Sozon's Cone, *Conus sozoni,* 2-4", SC to K, G.

Alphabet Cone, *Conus spurius atlanticus,* 2-3", F, G.

Crown Cone, *Conus regius,* 2-3", SF, WI.

Glory-of-the-Atlantic Cone, *Conus granulatus,* 1-1¾", SEF, WI.

Conus floridanus burryae, 1½-1¾", F.

Conus pygmaeus, 1-1½", F, WI.

Florida Cone, *Conus floridanus,* 1½-1¾", NC, F.

Stimpson's Cone, *Conus stimpsoni,* 1½-2", SEF, G.

Conus ranunculus, 2-3", F, WI.

Sennott's Cone, *Conus sennottorum,* 1-1½", G.

ʉse Cone, *Conus* s,1-1½", SEF, WI.

Carrot Cone, *Conus daucus,* 1-2", F, WI.

Dark Florida Cone, *Conus floridanus floridensis,* 1½-1¾", F.

Julia's Cone, *Conus juliae,* 1½-2", NEF to Tortugas.

Olives and Marginellas

Netted Olive, *Oliva reticularis,* 1½-2″, SEF, WI.

Oliva reticularis olorinella, 1½″-1¾″, C.

Orange Marginella, *Prunum carneum,* ¾″, SEF, WI.

West Indian Dwarf Olive, *Olivella nivea,* ½-1″, SEF, WI.

White-spotted Marginella, *Prunum guttatum,* ½-¾″, SEF, WI.

Oliva reticularis greenwayi, 1½″-2″, B.

Oliva reticularis bollingi, 1½-1¾″, B.

Lettered Olive, *Oliva sayana,* 2-2½″, NC to F, G.

Turrets, Spindles and Vase Shells

1. **Chestnut Latirus,** *Leucozonia nassa,* 1½″, F, WI,
2. **Caribbean Vase Shell,** *Vasum muricatum,* 2½-4″, SF, WI.
3. *Crassispira sanibelensis,* 1″, SF.
4. **McGinty's Latirus,** *Latirus mcgintyi,* ½-2½″, SEF.
5. **Spiny Vase Shell,** *Vasum capitellus,* 2-3″, Puerto Rico and Lesser Antilles.
6. **Giant White Turret,** *Polystira albida,* 3-4″, SF, G, WI.
7. **Delicate Giant Turret,** *Polystira tellea,* 3-3½″, SEF.
8. **Elegant Star Turret,** *Ancistrosyrinx elegans,* 2″, KW.
9. **Short-tailed Latirus,** *Latirus brevicaudatus,* 1-2½″, K, WI.
10. **White-spotted Latirus,** *Leucozonia ocellata,* 1″, F, WI.
11. *Latirus cymatius,* 1″, F.

Volutes

Worm Shells, Trivias and Periwinkles

1. **West Indian Worm Shell,** *Vermicularia spirata,* 3-6", SEF, WI.
2. **Common Prickly-winkle,** *Nodilittorina tuberculata,* ½-¾", SF, WI.
3. **Slit Worm Shell,** *Siliquaria squamatus,* 5-6", SEF, WI.
4. **Beaded Periwinkle,** *Tectarius muricatus,* ½-1", K, WI.
5. **Florida Worm Shell,** *Vermicularia knorri,* 3-6", NC, F, G.
6. **Coffee Bean Trivia,** *Trivia pediculus,* ½", SF, WI.
7. **Suffuse Trivia,** *Trivia suffusa,* ¼-1/3", SEF, WI.

◄

1. **Kiener's Volute,** *Scaphella kieneri,* 5-8", G.
2. *Scaphella cuba,* 2", Cuba, Florida Straits.
3. *Scaphella georgiana,* 3-4", Georgia, FEC.
4. **Music Volute,** *Voluta musica,* 2-2½", C.
5. *Scaphella gouldiana,* 2-3", F.
6. Smaller specimen *Scaphella kieneri.*
7. **Dubious Volute,** *Scaphella dubia,* 3-4", SF, G.
8. **Dohrn's Volute,** *Scaphella dohrni,* 3-4", SF.

Other Univalves

1. **Gaudy Cantharus,** *Cantharus auritula,* ¾-1¼", SEF, WI.
2. **Common Slipper Shell,** *Crepidula fornicata,* ¾-2", Canada to F, T.
3. *Nassarius hotessieri,* ¼-½", G.
4. **Dove Shell,** *Columbella mercatoria,* ½-¾", SEF, WI.
5. **West Indian Cup and Saucer,** *Crucibulum auricula,* 1", WF, K, WI.
6. **Variable Nassa,** *Nassarius consensus,* ½", F, WI.

1. **Lamellose Wentletrap,** *Epitonium lamellosum,* ¾-1¼", SF, C.
2. **Cancellate Cantharus,** *Cantharus cancellaria,* ¾-1¼", WF to T, Y.
3. **Arrow Dwarf Triton,** *Colubraria lanceolata,* ¾-1", F, WI.
4. **Giant Atlantic Pyram,** *Pyramidella dolabrata,* ¾-1", B, WI.

Tinted Cantharus,
Cantharus tinctus,
¾-1¼", F, WI.

Royal Florida Miter, *Mitra florida,* 1½-2", SF, WI.

Niso hendersoni, 1",
Southeastern U.S.

Colubraria testacea, ½-1½",
Tortugas, WI.

Boring Turret, *Turritella acropora,* 1-2", F, WI.

Eastern Turret, *Turritella exoleta,* 2", SF, WI.

Clams

Atlantic Surf Clam, *Spisula solidissima similis,* up to 7", Eastern U.S.

1. Gibb's Clam, *Eucrassatella speciosa,* 1½-2½", NC, F, WI.
2. Smooth Duck Clam, *Labiosa lineata,* 2-3", NC to NF.
3. Carolina Marsh Clam, *Polymesoda caroliniana,* 1-1½", V to NF, T.
4. *Tivela mactroides,* 1½-2½", K, WI.

1. Channeled Duck Clam, *Labiosa plicatella,* 2-3", NC, F, T, WI.
2. Green Jackknife Clam, *Solen viridis,* 2", Rhode Island to NF, G.
3. Jackknife Clam, *Ensis minor,* 2-3", F to T.
4. Corrugated Razor Clam, *Solecurtus cumingianus,* 1-2", F, G.

Scallops and Pectens

1. **Ravenel's Scallop,** *Pecten raveneli,* 1-2", G, WI.
2. **Rough Scallop,** *Aequipecten muscosus,* ¾-1¼", F, WI.
3. **Little Knobby Scallop,** *Chlamys imbricatus,* 1-1¾", SEF, WI.

1. **Spathate Scallop,** *Aequipecten phrygium,* 1",, CC to EF, WI.
2. **Sentis Scallop or Thorn Pecten,** *Chlamys sentis,* 1-1¼", NC to SEF, WI.
3. **Antillean Scallop,** *Lyropecten antillarum,* ½-¾", F, WI.
4. **Benedict's Scallop,** *Chlamys benedicti,* ¼-½", SF, G.

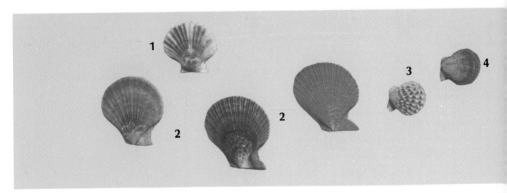

1. *Pecten irradians amplicostatus,* 2-3", G.
2. **Tereinus Scallop,** *Pecten tereinus,* 1", SF, G.
3. **Atlantic Bay Scallop,** *Aequipecten irradians,* 2-3", Nova Scotia to F.
4. **Calico Scallop,** *Aequipecten gibbus,* 1-2", G, WI.
5. **Wavy-lined Scallop,** *Aequipecten lineolaris,* 1-2", K to LA.

Pectens and Scallops

1. **Mildred's Scallop,** *Chlamys mildredae,* 1-1¼", SEF, BR.
2. **Atlantic Deep-sea Scallop,** *Placopecten magellanicus,* 5-8", Eastern U.S.
3. *Pecten laurenti,* 2½", GA.
4. **Zigzag Scallop,** *Pecten ziczac,* 2-4", NC to F, WI.
5. **Tryon's Scallop,** *Aequipecten glyptus,* 1-2½", CC to G.
6. **Ornate Scallop,** *Chlamys ornatus,* 1-1¼", SEF, WI.
7. **Paper Scallop,** *Pecten papyraceus,* Gabb, 2", G, WI.

Lion's Paw, *Pecten nodosus,* 3-6", NC, F, WI.

Angel Wings

1. **Angel Wing,** *Cyrtopleura costata,* 4-8", Massachusetts to F, T, WI.
2. **Campeche Angel Wing,** *Pholas campechiensis,* 3-4", NC to G, Central America.
3. **Fallen Angel Wing,** *Barnea truncata,.* 2-2½", Massachusetts, to SF.

Arks

1. **White Bearded Ark,** *Barbatia candida,* 1½-2½", NC to Brazil.
2. **Cut-ribbed Ark,** *Anadara lienosa floridana,* 2½-5", NC, F to T, GA.
3. **Doc Bale's Ark,** *Barbatia tenera,* 1-1½", SF to T, C.
4. **Incongruous Ark,** *Anadara brasiliana,* 1-2½", NC to WF, WI.

1. **Red-brown Ark,** *Barbatia cancellaria,* 1-1½", SF, WI.
2. *Anadara secticostata,* 2½-5", F, WI.
3. **Eared Ark,** *Anadara notabilis,* 1½-3½", NF to C, Brazil.
4. **Ponderous Ark,** *Noetia ponderosa,* 2-2½", South Atlantic Coast, F, G.
5. **Turkey Wing,** *Arca zebra,* 2-3", NC to LA.
6. **Mossy Ark,** *Arca umbonata,* 1½-2½", NC to WI.
7. **Blood Ark,** *Anadara ovalis,* Brug, 1½-2½", CC to WI, G.

Cockles

1. **Morton's Egg Cockle,** *Laevicardium mortoni,* ¾-1" CC to F. WI.
2. **and 3. Prickly Cockle or Rose Cockle,** *Trachycardium egmontianum,* 2", NC to SF, WI.
4. **Atlantic Strawberry Cockle,** *Trigoniocardia media,* 1-2", F, WI.
5. **Common Egg Cockle,** *Laevicardium laevigatum,* 1-2", NC to F, WI.
6. **Magnum Cockle,** *Trachycardium magnum,* 2-3½", K, WI.
7. **Giant Atlantic Cockle,** *Dinocardium robustum,* 3-4", V to NF, T, Mexico.
8. **Ravenel's Egg Cockle,** *Laevicardium pictum,* ½-1", South Carolina to SEF, WI.
9. **Spiny Paper Cockle,** *Papyridea soleniformis,* 1-1¾", F, WI.
10. **Lemon or Yellow Cockle,** *Trachycardium muricatum,* 2", NC to F, T, WI.
11. **Common Heart Cockle,** *Dinocardium robustum vanhyningi,* 3½-5", WF.
12. **West Indies Prickly Cockle,** *Trachycardium isocardia,* 2-3", WI.

Venus Clams

1. **Beaded Venus,** *Chione granulata*, ¾-1¼", WI.
2. **Quahog Clam,** *Mercenaria mercenaria*, 3-5", F, G.
3. **King Venus,** *Chione paphia*, 1½", K, WI.
4. **Rigid Venus,** *Antigona rigida*, (also *Ventricolaria rigida*), 1½-2½", WI.
5. **Elegant Dosinia,** *Dosinia elegans*, Conrad, 2-3", WF to T.
6. *Chione mazycki*, Dall, 1-1½", Carolinas, Georgia, N.E. Florida.
7. **Calico Clam,** *Macrocallista maculata*, 1½-2½", F, WI.
8. **Empress Venus,** *Antigona strigillina*, 1½", SEF, WI.
9. **Royal Comb Venus,** *Pitar dione*, Linne, 1-1¾", T to Panama, WI.
10. **Sunray Venus,** *Macrocallista nimbosa*, 4-5", F, G.
11. **Lady-in-Waiting Venus,** *Chione intapurpurea*, 1-1½", NC, G, WI.
12. **Imperial Venus,** *Chione latilirata*, 1", NC to F, T.
13. **Pointed Venus,** *Anomalocardia cuneimeris*, Conrad, ½-¾", SF to T.
14. **Glory-of-the-sea Venus,** *Callista eucymata*, 1-1½", North Carolina to SF, T, WI.
15. **Queen Venus,** *Antigona rugatina*, (also *Ventricolaria rugatina*), 1-1½", SEF, WI.
16. **Cross-barred Venus,** *Chione cancellata*, 1-1¾", NC to F, WI.
17. **Princess Venus,** *Periglypta listeri*, 2-4", SEF, WI.

Oysters

1. *Ostrea cristata,* 1-2″, C.
2. **Crested Oyster,** *Ostrea equestris,* 1-2″, F, G, WI.
3. **Atlantic Pearl Oyster,** *Pinctada radiata,* Leach, 1½-3″, SF, WI.
4. **Atlantic Wing Oyster,** *Pteria colymbus,* 1½-3″, NC, SEF, WI.
5. **Lister's Tree Oyster,** *Isognomon radiatus,* ½-2″, SEF, WI.
6. **Flat Tree Oyster,** *Isognomon alatus,* 2-3″, SF, WI.
7. **Coon Oyster,** *Ostrea frons,* 1-2″, F, Louisiana, WI.
8. **Sponge Oyster,** *Ostrea permollis,* 1-3″, F, WI.

Mussels

1. **Spiny Lima,** *Lima lima,* 1-1½", SEF, WI.
2. **Scorched Mussel,** *Brachidontes exustus,* ¾", NC to WI.
3. *Lima scabra tenera,* 1-3", SEF, WI.
4. **Giant Date Mussel,** *Lithophaga antillarum,* 2-4", G, WI.
5. **Hooked Mussel,** *Brachidontes recurvus,* 1-2½", CC to WI.
6. **Scissor Date Mussel,** *Lithophaga aristata,* ½-1", SF, WI.
7. **Tulip Mussel,** *Modiolus americanus,* 1-4", NC to WI.

Lucines and Bittersweets

1. **Chalky Buttercup Shell,** *Anodontia schrammi,* 2-4″, NC to EF, Cuba, BR.
2. **Comb Bittersweet,** *Glycymeris pectinata,* ½-1″, NC, F, WI.
3. **Pennsylvania Lucine,** *Lucina pennsylvanica,* 1-2″, F, WI.
4. **Northeast Lucine,** *Lucina filosus,* 1-3″, Newfoundland to NF, G.
5. **Decussate Bittersweet,** *Glycymeris decussata,* 2″, SEF, WI.
6. **Cross-hatched Lucine,** *Divaricella quadrisulcata,* ½-1″, Massachusetts to SF, WI.
7. **Thick Lucine,** *Lucina pectinatus,* 1-2½″, NC to F, G, WI.
8. **Tiger Lucine,** *Codakia orbicularis,* 2½-3½″, F to T, WI.
9. **Buttercup Lucine,** *Anodontia alba,* 1½-2″, NC to F, G, WI.
10. **Florida Lucine,** *Lucina floridana,* 1½″, G.
11. **Giant American Bittersweet,** *Glycymeris americana,* up to 5″, NC to NF, T.

Jewel Boxes and Spiny Oysters

1. *Spondylus gussoni,* 2-4", G.
2. **White Smoothed-edged Jewel Box,** *Chama sinuosa,* 1-3", SF, WI.
3. **Little Corrugated Jewel Box,** *Chama congregata,* ½-1", F, WI.
4. **True Spiny Jewel Box,** *Echinochama arcinella,* 1-1½", NC to F, T.
5. **Leafy Jewel Box,** *Chama macerophylla,* 1-3", SEF, WI.

Atlantic Thorny Oyster, *Spondylus americanus,* 3-4", SF, WI.

Tellins and Semeles

Sunrise Tellin, *Tellina radiata,* 2-4", South Carolina to F, WI.

1. **Atlantic Grooved Macoma,** *Psammotreta intastriata,* 2-3", SF, C.
2. **Faust Tellin,** *Arcopagia fausta,* 2-4", NC to SEF, WI.
3. **Speckled Tellin,** *Tellina listeri,* 2½-3½", F, WI.
4. **Gaudy Asaphis,** *Asaphis deflorata,* 2", SEF, WI.
5. *Psammacola tagiliformis,* 1-2½", G.
6. **Smooth Tellin,** *Tellina laevigata,* 2-3", SF, WI.
7. **Great Tellin,** *Tellina magna,* 3-4½", NC to F, WI.

1. **Constricted Macoma,** *Macoma constricta,* 1-2½", F, WI.
2. **Large Strigilla,** *Strigilla carnaria,* ¾-1", F, WC.
3. **Cancellate Semele,** *Semele bellastriata,* ½-¾", F, WI.
4. **Crenulate Tellin,** *Phylloda squamifera,* ½-1", NC to SF.
5. **Alternate Tellin,** *Tellina alternata,* 2-3", NC to F, G.
6. **Crystal Tellin,** *Tellina cristallina,* ¾-1", South Carolina to WI.
7. **Candy-stick Tellin,** *Tellina similis,* 1", SF, B, WC.
8. **Rose Petal Tellin,** *Tellina lineata,* 1½", F, WI.
9. **Purplish Semele,** *Semele purpurascens,* 1-1¼", F, WI.
10. **White-crested Tellin,** *Tellidora cristata,* 1-1½", NC to WF, T.
11. **Purplish Tagelus,** *Tagelus divisus,* 1-1½", CC to SF, G, C.

Other Bivalves

Goeduck Shell, *Panope bitruncata,* 5-6", NC to F.

1. **False Angel Wing,** *Petricola pholadiformis,* 2", G.
2. **Jingle Shell,** *Anomia simplex,* 1-2", N.Y. to F, G, WI.
3. **Broad-ribbed Cardita,** *Cardita floridana,* 1-1½", SF.
4. **Kitten's Paw,** *Plicatula gibbosa,* 1", NC to G, WI.
5. **Common Coquina,** *Donax variabilis,* ½-¾", V to SF, T.

Atlantic Rupellaria, *Rupellaria typica,* 1″, F, WI.

Rocellaria ovata, ½-¾″, B, Atlantic Coast.

Donax denticulata, 1″, Southwestern Caribbean.

Stiff Pen Shell, *Atrina rigida,* 5-9″, NC to SF, C.

Giant False Donax, *Iphigenia brasiliensis,* 2-2½″, SF, WI.

Other Specimens

1. **Common Paper Nautilus,** *Argonauta argo,* 4-8".
2. **Common Spirula,** *Spirula spirula,* ½-1".
3. **Brown Paper Nautilus,** *Argonauta hians,* 2-3".

Cross section, **Chambered Nautilus,** *Nautilus macrophalus,* 6-8".

Sea fans,
Rhipigorgia flabellum,
all sizes.

Common West Indian Chiton, *Chiton tuberculatus,* 2-3".

Ivory Tusk Shell, *Dentalium eboreum,* 1-2½".

1. **Lace Sea Fan**, *Gorgonia,* many species, all sizes.
2. **Horseshoe Crab**, *Xiphosurus sowerbyi,* Maine to WI.
3. **California Starfish.** Class: *Asteroidea.* Many species.
4. **Florida Sand Dollar.** Class: *Echinoidea.* Many species, 1-4".
5. **Florida Sand Dollar.** Class: *Echinoidea.* Many species, 1-4".
6. **Mexican Sand Dollar.** Class: *Echinoidea.* Many species, 1-4".
7. **Florida Arrowhead Sand Dollar.** Class: *Echinoidea.* Many species, 1-4".
8. **Millepeda Starfish.** Class: *Asteroidea.* Many species, 3-6".
9. **Cowfish**, *Lactophys tricornis,* 3-6".
10. **Pygmy Seahorse**, *Hippocampus zosterae,* less than 1".
11. **Florida Seahorse**, *Hippocampus hudsonicus,* 1-5".
12. **Brown Starfish.** Class: *Asteroidea.* Many species, 2-3".
13. **Small Florida Starfish**, *Asteracanthion vulgaris,* 1-2".
14. Variety of **Starfish.**
15. Denuded **Sea Urchin,** *Arbacia punctulata.*
16. **Giant Starfish**, *Pentaceros reticularis,* 6-12".
17. **Sea Biscuit,** species of Sea Urchin.
18. **Sea Urchin**, *Strongylocentratus drobachiensis.*

60

Index to Common Names

UNIVALVES

BIVALVES

Index to Scientific Names

CLASS GASTROPODA: UNIVALVES

CLASS PELECYPODA: BIVALVES

CLASS CEPHALOPODA: SQUID, OCTOPUS AND CUTTLEFISH

CLASS AMPHINEURA: CHITONS

CLASS SCAPHOPODA: DENTALIUMS AND OTHER TUSK SHELLS

MISCELLANEOUS CLASSES